POINT BLANK

POINT BLANK

By **IN YER FACE**

Christian Theatre Company

20 CUTTING EDGE DRAMAS TO PROVOKE AND CHALLENGE

Scripture Union

Scripture Union,
207–209 Queensway, Bletchley,
MK2 2EB, England.
www.scriptureunion.org.uk

Scripture Union is an international
Christian charity working with
churches in more than 130 countries,
providing resources to bring the
good news about Jesus Christ to children,
young people and families –
and to encourage them to develop
spiritually through the Bible and prayer.

As well as our network of volunteers,
staff and associates who run holidays,
church-based events and school
Christian groups, we produce a wide range
of publications and support those who use
resources through training programmes.

....

....

PERFORMING LICENCE

....

....

British Library
Cataloguing-in-Publication Data
A catalogue record for this book is
available from the British Library.

....

Cover design, Internal design and
Photography by Phil Grundy:

phil_451f@hotmail.com

....

Printed and bound by
Interprint Ltd, Malta

INDEX THEMES & BIBLE VERSES

CONTENTS PAGE

Have you ever watched a thoroughly entertaining and amusing drama as part of a youth service or church event but then experienced a slightly embarrassing and niggling feeling that you didn't actually know what it was about?

We are living amongst a generation of young people who receive their entertainment and amusement from computer games and videos but who never actually hear the Gospel.

Drama is an amazing medium if used effectively. Our aim is to use it to inform lost generations of their need for forgiveness and redemption, through the offer of Jesus Christ. Therefore, our dramas should entertain and amuse, but most importantly inform. The point must be clear and unmissable, leaving the audience in no doubt of the choices they must make.

We have sought to write dramas that do just that, their messages hitting audiences point blank in the forehead and seeping straight to the heart. I hope you enjoy reading them, but most importantly I hope you enjoy performing them and furthering the Kingdom of our Lord Jesus Christ.

God bless

Rik Brown (Artistic Director)
In Yer Face Christian Theatre Company

THINGS TO REMEMBER

If you are reading this having experienced a negative view of drama and a reluctance to see it as a fully-fledged gift, then take heart; we experience this too. However, we continue to see God using drama as a powerful and awesome evangelistic tool. We have seen how it is used to break down the hardest of hearts and to lead the lost home.

We have come to realise from experience that the more rehearsal, the better the performance, the less the hurdles a person has to overcome to see the life-changing message we are presenting to them.

To us as performers and writers, there is nothing better than someone coming up to us and saying, 'That drama really touched me,' 'I felt God really speaking to me through that drama,' 'I became a Christian,' 'I sorted my Christian life out,' 'I found God.' This is what we hear; not because we're anything special but because we serve an awesome God, and use our gifts to the fullest extent so his name may be proclaimed - as Jesus said, 'Go out and do likewise'.

A final point - a number of our sketches include 'Jesus' as a character. It is always wise when playing Jesus not to play him in a 'holy' manner - we have noticed the effectiveness of keeping the character of Jesus whenever portrayed as real as possible and preferably in modern dress.

From All at In Yer Face

Living in

CHARACTERS

Girl/Boy – young, likeable and trendy
Jesus

PROPS

Cross, blood-stained white T-shirt, music

ADDITIONAL INFORMATION

Jesus mimes as if the assault/crucifixion occurs directly through the girl/boy's words.
The girl/boy is oblivious to Jesus' presence.

Girl/Boy: (Listening to song playing.)
Great song that, isn't it?

(Jesus enters behind and stands at the foot of the cross.)

Girl/Boy: (To audience.)
What? What is it? Boo! You lot look like you're sat in church or something! Always found those places a bit weird myself. I mean, come on – a load of people getting together to listen to some bloke go on for hours about 'Thou shalt not do this' and 'Thou shalt not do that'. Waste of time, if you ask me.

(Jesus takes a punch to the stomach.)

Girl/Boy: Don't get me wrong – if that's what turns you on, that's fine. I'd just rather be doing something useful like seeing my mates... well, probably recovering from seeing my mates the night before, actually! I'm probably painting a bad picture of myself, aren't I? But I'm not a bad person, you know.

(Jesus takes a punch to the head.)

Girl/Boy: I guess I pray and stuff. Well, everyone does, don't they? It's like, if you walk down the high street, and you spot the bloke selling the Big Issue, and you say, 'O God! Please don't let him notice me! Let him pick on someone else!' Oh come on, don't look at me like that, we all do it. You gotta look after number one, haven't you?

(Jesus throws his left arm up.)

OBLIVION

Girl/Boy: And if he does catch up with you, he never has change. (Stares at audience.) What now? You're making me paranoid staring at me like that. Stop being so serious – you look like you're in church again! That's the other thing about churches – they're always trying to make you feel guilty about something. Well, I haven't done anything wrong.

(Jesus throws his right arm up.)

Girl/Boy: Well, all right, I might've done the odd thing I'm not too proud of, but does that mean I'm going to hell? And who the hell came up with that one, anyway? Who came up with all of this, for that matter? And don't tell me it was God or something, cos he doesn't exist.

(Jesus screams.)

Girl/Boy: This geek came knocking on my door the other day trying to tell me about Jesus and stuff. Well, I might not have loads of qualifications, like, but I'm not stupid! If you ask me, that Jesus was a nice bloke and everything, but he must've lost it somewhere down the line. Son of God? Cuckoo!

(Jesus' head falls.)

Girl/Boy: It's like my auntie. She thought she was Elvis Presley, but it doesn't mean she was. If you want my opinion, not that you asked, but I'll tell you anyway, life's got its ups and its downs, hasn't it? If I get knocked down, I get up again. You gotta roll with it, know what I mean? God? What's he ever done for me?

Jesus: Father, forgive them, for they know not what they do.

BIBLE

ISAIAH **28:16** (Trusting God's cornerstone – Jesus)
. . . .

QUESTIONS

What is the difference between the foundation in the verse and the girl/boy's foundation in the drama?

Which is the stronger foundation to build a life on and why?

How would you convince the character that God's foundation is better than hers/his?

THE END

CHARACTERS

Girl (or Boy) – young, trendy, unprepared for this situation

Death – authoritative, bleak, enjoys his job

PROPS

Handcuffs and a cross

ADDITIONAL INFORMATION

Change the name and biographical information in the sketch to fit the actor.

(Girl laughs.)

Death: Funny, isn't it?

Girl: What?

Death: I mean, you never know when it's coming.

Girl: What are you talking about?

Death: You see, people like to think they can laugh in my face, but it always ends up the other way around.

Girl: Who are you?

Death: Questions, questions... No answers, I'm afraid. You seemed so certain before, but look at you now.

Girl: Look, I'd love to chat, but I've got things to do. Excuse me.

Death: No, I can't. Anyway, I'm afraid it's too late for that. I've come to collect what's due.

Girl: I don't owe you anything!

Death: Oh, but you do.

Girl: Listen, mate, you've obviously got the wrong person.

Death: Then I'm sorry, and leave with my blessings... Sarah Elizabeth Howard.

Girl: Oh, I get it – it's a joke, right? I've been set up!

Death: Born: 20.02.74, Tameside Hospital. Height: 5'7. Weight: 9 stone 7. Marital Status: single. Educated: Manchester University. Current Position: unemployed. No distinguishing marks. It's a joke, right?

Girl: I don't understand.

Death: You will.

Girl: I haven't got time for this.

Death: Oh, but you have! There's no hurry. Not anymore.

Girl: Who are you?

Death: You know who I am.

Girl: No, I don't.

Death: Think about it.

Girl: None of this makes any sense.

Death: Life's a bit like that, so I'm told. Sometimes things just happen which seem so unfair. Lonely Valentines, lost kittens, cruel words in the playground, the ozone layer – I mean, what's that all about? Earthquakes, famines, floods, car crashes, plane crashes, train crashes, shouting, screaming, bleeding, dying...

Girl: You're sick.

Death: Thank you. But you're much worse, believe me.

Girl: Yeah? Well, I don't believe you.

Death: I find your lack of faith invigorating.

Girl: Do you? Good for you!

Death: Indeed. But bad for you. (Pause.) Anyway, enough talk. (Brings out handcuffs.)

Girl: What are you doing?

Death: Taking what's mine.

Girl: I don't belong to anyone but me!

Death: Wrong, wrong! You belong to me now. You chose me.

Girl: But I don't even know who you are!

Death: Death. Pleased to meet you. (The girl faints.) **Oh, I'm sorry, I seem to have this affect on people. Here, sit down.**
(Death catches her and spins her around onto a chair, handcuffing her to it.)

Girl: I don't deserve to die!

Death: Have died, have died, let's get our grammar correct.

Girl: I don't deserve this!

Death: Wrong again, I'm afraid.

Girl: I never had a hope...

Death: Oh, but you did.

Girl: Well, no one told me!

Death: He sent people to tell you, but you were too clever to listen.

Girl: Who?

Death: He sent you letters.

Girl: Who?

Death: He even sent his son to tell you in person, but you still didn't listen.

Girl: Who?!

(Death mimics the crucifixion.)

Death: Ring any bells?

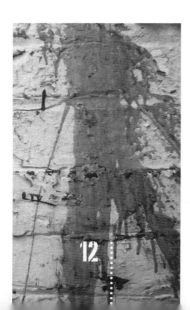

Girl: Oh my God!

Death: Exactly.

Girl: But I never realised –

Death: It doesn't matter now.

Girl: But there was so much else on offer!

Death: I know, and you made your choice.

Girl: But some said he was a liar –

Death: Is that why you killed him?

Girl: But I didn't kill anyone!

Death: Yes, you did! You hated and rejected him to the very end.

Girl: But if I'd known it was him –

Death: (Mimicking her.) 'But if I'd known it was him.'
Well, no more 'buts'. Come on.

Girl: You can go to hell!

Death: Exactly. And do you know what the best part is?
You get to go right along with me!

(Death unlocks the handcuffs and exits with the girl.)

BIBLE

PROVERBS 14:12 (Living life your own way leads to death)
JOHN 6:39,40 (All who trust Jesus will be raised and have eternal life)

QUESTIONS

What is the girl's reaction to death?

The girl says, 'But there was so much else on offer!' How does this relate to the proverb?

According to God's promise in John's Gospel, how will the Christian's death differ from the girl's?

CHARACTERS

Bouncer – firm, but fair, good at his job
Girl – student, feisty, arrogant
Smith - student

PROPS

Cross, guest list, bouncer jacket, flyer, twenty-pound note, packet of cigarettes, lighter

ADDITIONAL INFORMATION

The sketch appears to take place outside a nightclub, but it becomes apparent it is outside the gates of heaven. The bouncer stands just in front of the cross.

THE GUEST

Girl:	All right... (Starts to walk past the bouncer.)
Bouncer:	Sorry, love, not tonight.
Girl:	What d'you mean?
Bouncer:	I mean you're not getting in.
Girl:	Is it cos I'm wearing trainers? I'll take them off, okay?
Bouncer:	No need, there's no dress code.
Girl:	Right, then... (Tries to go in again.)
Bouncer:	But you're still not getting in.
Girl:	Look, I am over twenty-one, you know.
Bouncer:	So I can see, but there's no age limit. Now, do me a favour and move along, will you?
Girl:	Wait a minute, my flyer says guaranteed entry.

Bouncer:	Really? And have you read the small print?
Girl:	What small print? It just says 'Guaranteed entry'.
Bouncer:	Yeah, 'Guaranteed entry before midnight'.
Girl:	But it's only five past!
Bouncer:	Well, that's five minutes too late in my book.
Girl:	Oh, come on, I'm sure your boss won't mind.
Bouncer:	And how would you know?
Girl:	Because I know him.
Bouncer:	Oh really? And how exactly do you know the boss?
Girl:	Let's just say we go back a long way...
Bouncer:	Well, I'll give him a shout then, shall I?

(Goes to shout him.)

Girl:	No! I mean, he probably won't recognise me, I used to have really short hair.
Bouncer:	How very convenient.
Girl:	Oh, this is stupid! Look, couldn't you just sneak me in round the back? I won't tell anyone.
Bouncer:	Sorry, love - there's only the one way in.
Girl:	All right, if this is what it comes down to...

(Holds out a twenty-pound note.)

LIST

Bouncer:	What's that?
Girl:	It's a twenty-pound note.
Bouncer:	So it is.
Girl:	Well, go on, then, take it!
Bouncer:	Thanks very much.
Girl:	Right. (Starts to go in.)
Bouncer:	Dunno what you're doing that for, you're still not getting in.
Girl:	What? You've just robbed me!
Bouncer:	No, I haven't. Here, have it back if it means that much to you.
Girl:	Oh, so my money's not good enough for you?
Bouncer:	You don't get it, do you?
Girl:	You know, I've met your sort before.
Bouncer:	Oh, here we go...
Girl:	You get a little bit of power and you think you're really something, don't you? Well you're just a bouncer, you know!
Bouncer:	And you're just not getting in, you know.
Girl:	Yeah? Well, we'll see about that. I know people...

(Goes to use her mobile.)

Bouncer: I'm shaking in my boots.

(Smith enters.)

Smith: Alright?

Bouncer: Alright, mate.

Smith: Here you go. (Gives him his invitation.)

Bouncer: Oh right. Hang on, I'll just get the list...
Now then, what name is it?

Smith: It's Smith.

Bouncer: Mmm... here we go – Mr Smith. Right, what you
need to do is take this to the bloke at the top of
the stairs, and he'll sort you out.

Smith: Cheers, mate. (Smith enters the club past the cross)

Girl: Hang on, it's after midnight!

Bouncer: So?

Girl: So how come you let him in?

Bouncer: He's on the list.

Girl: What list?

Bouncer: The guest list. Accepted personal invitations.

Girl: Well, I got an invite once.

Bouncer: Everybody gets an invite, but you mustn't have
taken him up on the offer, otherwise your name
would be on the list as well.

Girl: Yeah, well I had these other tickets to
somewhere nearer. I mean, you've got to admit
it's a bit of a hike up here.

Bouncer: Worth the walk, though.

Girl: How would I know? It's not exactly well advertised, is it?

Bouncer: It's all around, you just had to open your eyes.

Girl: So what's it like?

Bouncer: What? Here?

Girl: No, over there.

Bouncer: Dunno. Don't work over there.

Girl: No, what's it like here?

Bouncer: Well, think of the best there is, double it, quadruple it,
and you'll still be nowhere near. And the boss is a great bloke,
fairest in the business.

Girl: Well he's not being very fair now, is he?

Bouncer: (Getting fed up.) Oi listen! He invited you, right,
and you said 'no', and when you finally get around
to gracing us with your presence...
Well, I'm afraid it's too late. Your choice,
your problem, so don't start blaming the boss now.

Girl: Well you know what?

Bouncer: What?

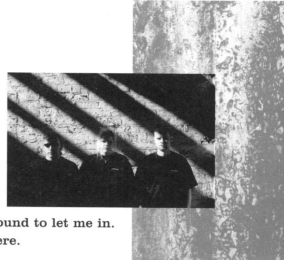

Girl:	I'm not bothered anyway.
Bouncer:	Oh really.
Girl:	Yeah. I'll just go somewhere else.
Bouncer:	There's only the one place open.
Girl:	Fine, I'll go there, then, they're bound to let me in.
Bouncer:	Yeah, sadly most people get in there.
Girl:	And d'you know the best bit?
Bouncer:	No, but I've got a feeling I'm going to find out.
Girl:	You can't stop me getting in there!
Bouncer:	I wish I could.
Girl:	I bet you do. Oh, by the way, I just wanted to say 'thanks'.
Bouncer:	Thanks? For what?
Girl:	For nothing! (She exits.)
Bouncer:	(Sadly.) Enjoy yourself.

BIBLE

MATTHEW 25:1-13 (THE PARABLE OF THE TEN VIRGINS AND THE WEDDING BANQUET)

....

QUESTIONS

WHY ARE THE GIRL'S ATTEMPTS TO GET INTO HEAVEN UNSUCCESSFUL?

WHAT IS THE MESSAGE PRESENTED BY BOTH THE PARABLE AND THE SKETCH?

WHAT CAN WE DO TO MAKE SURE OUR FRIENDS ARE ON GOD'S GUEST LIST?

LIVING IN OBLIVION, THE END AND THE GUEST LIST CAN BE PERFORMED ONE AFTER THE OTHER. IF YOU CHOOSE TO DO THIS, THE GIRL NEEDS TO GET AWAY FROM DEATH AT THE CONCLUSION OF THE END, SO SHE CAN APPEAR IN THE GUEST LIST.

MAN UPSTAIRS

CHARACTERS

Dealer - streetwise
Clubber - young, trendy, searching

PROPS

Bible or hand-held cross

ADDITIONAL INFORMATION

Try to create an overall feel that suggests a drug deal.

Dealer: Alright.
Clubber: Alright, what's happening?
Dealer: Got something special for ya.
Clubber: Yeah? What is it?
Dealer: The best.
Clubber: Something new?
Dealer: Not exactly.
Clubber: I just wanna get wasted.
Dealer: This'll do better than that.
Clubber: Yeah?
Dealer: Yeah. Once you've taken it, you'll never come down.
Clubber: Sounds good. But how high do you get?
Dealer: This stuff'll really take you there.
Clubber: I'm not just gonna take anything, you know.
Dealer: Trust me.

(Pause.)

Clubber: Who's your dealer?
Dealer: The main man.
Clubber: What? You don't mean...
Dealer: Yeah...
Clubber: Forget it. His stuff is bad. It really screws you up!
Dealer: Who told you that?
Clubber: The word's on the street.
Dealer: Have you ever tried it for yourself?
Clubber: Well... no, but I've seen what it does to people.
Dealer: Yeah? What's that?

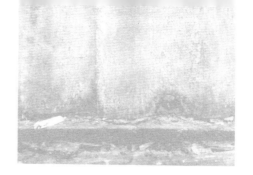

Clubber: They've totally lost it!

Dealer: Isn't that what you want?

Clubber: No... Yes... I just wanna get out of it!

Dealer: Oh, this stuff'll do that all right – it's like nothing else around.

Clubber: So how do you actually take it?

Dealer: Straight in the heart.

Clubber: But if it's as good as you say it is, how come I haven't heard of it before?

Dealer: Well, a lot of users keep it to themselves. C'mon, what've you got to lose?

Clubber: What if I OD?

Dealer: No chance.

Clubber: But I could die!

Dealer: That's why you should take it. Go on, try it.

Clubber: Okay, okay... Hold on – how much is this gonna cost me?

Dealer: Get this – it's already paid for. It's being given away.

Clubber: Yeah, sure. C'mon, how much?

Dealer: Like I said, it's totally free!

Clubber: That's it. This is too much! Some losers might fall for it, but not this one! Nothing's as good as that, and nothing's ever free. Just forget it, will ya?

Dealer: Fair enough, your decision. But I'm telling you, it's your loss. Then again, maybe you're right – I mean life's not that bad, is it? You enjoy it... (Pause.) (To the audience) **Wanna get high?** (Pulls out Bible or cross and offers it to the audience.)

BIBLE

MARK 8:34,35 (Save your life by losing it to the gospel)

QUESTIONS

What reasons does the man give for not accepting what he's offered?

In the passage, Jesus talks about picking up the cross. Why does the man in the drama reject it?

Is Christianity the ultimate high?

Jesus paid the price, but what is the cost of following him?

CHARACTERS

Girl – idealistic, school-aged pupil
Boy – cynical, school-aged pupil

PROPS

None

ADDITIONAL INFORMATION

Best in a contemporary setting.

Points OF View

Girl: You fancy that Nina Smith, don't you? (Pause.) I said, you fancy...

Boy: I heard what you said.

Girl: Well, do you?

Boy: No. I don't.

Girl: Are you in love with her?

Boy: No. (Pause.) I don't believe in any of that.

Girl: What do you mean?

Boy: Look, my dad says he loves my mum, then he comes home drunk and boots her across the kitchen... And my auntie, she says she loves my uncle Derek ... and his best mate... and the bloke next door.

Girl: Yeah? Well, my sister's in love. She's getting married.

Boy: Oh, so does that mean she loves him? Just cos she puts on a stupid dress and gets confetti in her hair?

Girl: Well, if love doesn't exist, why are so many songs written about it?

Boy: Cos people want it to exist.

Girl: Well, my grandparents are in love. They're seventy and they're still going strong. My grandad's deaf and pig ugly, that means she must love him!

Boy: No, it doesn't.

Girl: What do you mean?

Boy: It's just habit. They've been together so long they wouldn't know how to function on their own. (Pause.) It's like smoking – they need each other, like your old man needs a cigarette.

Girl: Look, love must exist – it's in the dictionary.

Boy: Yeah? So's wind, but you can't see it.

Girl: Yeah, but you can see its effects...

Boy: Well, the only effect you can see from love is pain. My mum sat crying and my uncle Derek's going out of his mind, wondering where his wife is tonight.

Girl: But we know hate exists, cos I hate my brother.

Boy: So what's your point?

Girl: Well, it's like black and white, life and death – you can't have one without the other.

(Boy laughs.)

Girl: What is the point, then?

Boy: What do you mean?

Girl: If there isn't love, what's the point in anything?

Boy: There isn't one.

BIBLE

1 JOHN 4:7-10
(GOD'S LOVE AND OURS)

QUESTIONS

WHAT ARE THE TWO CHARACTERS' POINTS OF VIEW ABOUT LOVE?

ACCORDING TO THE VERSES, HOW DOES GOD SHOW US WHAT LOVE IS?

HOW CAN AND SHOULD WE RESPOND TO GOD'S LOVE?

TRUE ROMANCE

CHARACTERS

Boy – likeable, Jack the Lad
Girl – likeable, assertive

PROPS

None

ADDITIONAL INFORMATION

The boy and girl have dated a while. The girl is tiring of the boy's empty words. The sketch ends with the boy in a crucifixion pose to illustrate Jesus' unconditional love on the cross.

Boy: Hey – I love you!

Girl: Do you?

Boy: Yeah, course I do.

Girl: How much?

Boy: Oh, I dunno, probably... (Stretches out hands.) This much!

Girl: No, I'm serious. How much?

Boy: What do you mean?

Girl: Well, you're always saying it...

Boy: Yeah – so?

Girl: Well, do you really mean it?

Boy: Yeah...

Girl: Then how much?

Boy: Well, I dunno... I love you loads. Is that enough?

Girl: Show me.

Boy: What?

Girl: Show me how much you love me.

Boy: All right, then, shut your eyes. (Kisses her.)

Girl: What are you doing?

Boy: I'm kissing you, what do you think I'm doing?

Girl: Why?

Boy: Cos I'm showing you how much I love you.

Girl: And how exactly does that show me?

Boy: Well, it shows you that I fancy you, doesn't it?

Girl: Oh great! That means you only love my body, not my mind.

Boy: Don't be daft, course I love your mind. (Stares at her body.)

Girl: Oi!

Boy: Sorry.

Girl: So what do you love about my mind?

Boy: Well... you make me laugh.

Girl: So does Teletubbies! I mean, it's hardly a compliment, is it?

Boy: Well, you make me think as well.

Girl: So does Countdown.

Boy: Oh, this is stupid! How am I supposed to show you that I love you?

Girl: That's the point – you can't!

Boy: Well, I never let you down, do I?

Girl: You're always late.

Boy: I never look at other women. (Spotting someone.) **Apart from you, luv. How you doing?**

(She kicks him.)

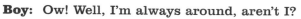

Boy: Ow! Well, I'm always around, aren't I?

Girl: So's the dog.

Boy: Well, he loves you!

Girl: No, he doesn't, he just wants feeding.

Boy: (Aside.) Yeah, so do I!

Girl: What?

Boy: Er... I'd save you if you were drowning.

Girl: You can't even swim.

Boy: Well, if you were stuck in a big building that was on fire, I'd climb up and rescue you.

Girl: You can't stand heights.

Boy: I'd cross a desert to be with you.

Girl: You got sunstroke at Blackpool.

Boy: Well, I'd... I'd... Oh, what's the point!

Girl: What do you mean?

Boy: I hate you when you're in this mood.

Girl: But you said you loved me...

Boy: I do... but not right now. (Pause.) Anyway, no one could live up to your expectations.

Girl: Why not?

Boy: No one could show you they loved you that much, I mean how on earth could they?

(Boy stretches out his arms, then bows his head to suggest the crucifixion.)

BIBLE

1 CORINTHIANS 13:4-7 (A DESCRIPTION OF TRUE LOVE)

QUESTIONS

How is love as defined in the verses different to the man's idea of love in the drama?

How did Jesus show he loved us?

Is your love more like that of the man in the drama or as it is described in the verses?

COFFIN FIT

(Character 2 messes with some wood as Character 1 enters.)

1: What are you doing?

2: What does it look like?

1: Dunno.

2: I'm thinking about the future.

1: Oh right. Sorry?

2: That's okay.

1: No – I mean, what are you doing?!

2: Preparing myself.

1: You're very into wood, aren't you?

2: I will be. What do you think? Antique pine or good old chestnut?
Can't beat a nice piece of chestnut, can you?

1: Er... no.

2: Hold this, will you. (Passes over the end of the tape measure.)

1: Are you all right?

2: Fine. For now. Be dead soon, though.

1: What?

2: I mean, we'll all be worm food soon, won't we?

1: Speak for yourself!

CHARACTERS

Character 1 – school-aged, fearful of death
Character 2 – school-aged, faces up to reality of death

PROPS

Two planks of wood, tape measure

ADDITIONAL INFORMATION

None

2: But we're all going to die, aren't we? Death comes to us all.

1: Don't say that word.

2: What word? 'Death'?

1: I said don't say it!

2: What's wrong with saying 'dea...' that word?

1: Well, because it's against the law.

2: What are you on about?

1: Me? What about you?

2: Don't you think it makes sense to be ready?

1: When I'm drawing my pension, then maybe, but there's so much else to think about in the meantime.

2: Yeah? Like what?

1: Well, like... er... oh, I don't know, there's just so much else going on, isn't there?

2: Places to go, people to see?

1: Exactly.

2: Well, don't let me stop you. I'll see you tomorrow.

1: Ah, but according to you tomorrow may not exist!

2: Precisely. (Exits.)

1: What?

BIBLE

1 CORINTHIANS 15:21,22 (Resurrection through Jesus)

QUESTIONS

How do the characters' preparations for death differ?

How does Jesus truly prepare us for death?

How should this affect our perceptions of living and dying?

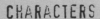

CHARACTERS

Learner – young, scatty
Instructor – uptight, edgy,
older than learner

PROPS

Clipboard for Instructor

ADDITIONAL INFORMATION

The sketch begins after the
driving test has ended.

Learner:	Well, that seemed to go pretty well!
Instructor:	Pretty well?!
Learner:	Yeah. What do you think?
Instructor:	What do I think? The only thing you did right was putting your seatbelt on!
Learner:	What do you mean?
Instructor:	Well, let's start at the beginning, shall we?
Learner:	All right, then. I s'pose it was a bit chuggy at first.
Instructor:	And why was that? Because you drove forty yards before you realised you'd left the handbrake on.
Learner:	Oh, is that what the smell of burning was?
Instructor:	No, that was the seat covers when you decided to light up during the emergency stop procedure. I mean, what did you think you were doing?
Learner:	When?
Instructor:	On the hill start, for example.
Learner:	Well, the thing was I couldn't find the clutch point, so I didn't notice we were rolling back – good job that car was there, though, eh?

Instructor:	What?
Learner:	Well, if we hadn't hit that, we'd have crashed into that blooming big bus.
Instructor:	You did crash into that 'blooming big bus'!
Learner:	No I didn't, that was later, and besides, that wasn't my fault.
Instructor:	Then who's fault was it?
Learner:	Paul's.
Instructor:	Paul's?

BENDS

Learner: Yeah, the bloke I was waving to. I mean, everyone knows you don't wave to people taking their test.

Instructor: All right, so who's fault was it that you ran three red lights and two unmarked crossroads?

Learner: Madonna's.

Instructor: Madonna's? Why was it her fault?

Learner: Because I can't concentrate properly if the graphic equalizer's not right – the tape sounds really tinny.

Instructor: You're not supposed to have tapes on during your test!

Learner: Well, I did wonder why I couldn't hear you properly. Look, did I pass on any part?

Instructor: Yes…

Learner: Oh good!

Instructor: You managed to shut the door… eventually.

Learner: But I didn't hit anybody

Instructor: Yes you did.

Learner: Well, not in a killing sort of way.

Instructor: We don't know that yet, do we?

Learner: So do you think we should phone the hospital about the old dear?

Instructor: Yes! And while you're at it, ask her if she wants her zimmer frame back.

Learner: Why? Have you got it?

Instructor: Of course I've got it! It's stuck on the front of the car! Didn't you see her?

Learner: No! Well, I felt the thud, but she looked all right when we drove off – she was waving.

Instructor: No she wasn't.

Learner: She was. Like this! (Goes to make a rude gesture.)

Instructor: That's quite enough, thank you. Just take it from me, it wasn't a wave. Anyway, I've got a question for you.

Learner: Oh, I've already got a boyfriend.

Instructor: (Looks shocked.) And I've already got a wife! Right. Imagine you're in the car, and this is me clinging to the dashboard. Now, what is the procedure when approaching a roundabout?

Learner: Oh roundabouts, I love them! Well, you get up to it, and then it's a bit like a game of British Bulldog – you have to get to the other side as fast as you can without getting caught.

Instructor: And did you win your game?

Learner: Not exactly, no. I got hit by that blasted car…

Instructor: Yes, and how you failed to see that 'blasted car' is beyond me. I rather thought the big blue flashing light on top of it made it instantly noticeable, but oh no, you go straight into the side of it, and into the middle of the roundabout!

Learner: Yes, well, it's safe in the middle, isn't it? They can't get you there. At least he didn't write us a ticket.

Instructor: No, but perhaps that's because you broke both his arms, and it took them three hours to cut him out of the wreckage. I mean, what were you thinking of? Why weren't you concentrating?!

Learner: (Thinking about something else.) **Sorry?**

Instructor: Oh, forget it.

Learner: Are you all right?

Instructor: No, I am not all right! Just tell me why... please!

Learner: Well, I was too busy driving the car to look at the road – every time I looked up, I suddenly remembered about the gears or the clutch or the steering wheel. Besides, there were too many distractions, my mind was on other things, and before I knew it, the test was over and I'd failed. Look, I'm sorry... What are you doing?

Instructor: Writing.

Learner: Have I passed?

Instructor: Here – your new test date: November 2nd. Everyone gets a second chance, even you. Just promise me one thing. Next time, you'll keep your eyes on the road and not get so easily distracted. (Exits.)

Learner: Don't know what his problem was – I mean, everyone gets distracted, not just me.

BIBLE

PHILIPPIANS 3:12-14
(Not perfect yet, but pressing on towards the goal)

....

QUESTIONS

What should the learner have done to pass the test?

How did Paul (who wrote Philippians) continue despite distractions?

What distracts you in your daily walk with God? What can you do about this?

THE MENU

CHARACTERS

Waiter – has an over the top French accent
Man and Woman – a downmarket couple going to an upmarket French restaurant for the night. They have no knowledge of French.

PROPS

Table, two chairs, two glasses, two menus, waiter's notepad, pen

ADDITIONAL INFORMATION

The table and chairs need to be on the stage, with the menus on the table, before the couple enter.

(Couple enter the restaurant.)

Waiter: Ah, bonsoir Monsieur, bonsoir Madame. Welcome to Le Restaurant les Péches. Please follow me.

Man: Thanks very much, er... garcon. (Pronounces it garkon.)

Waiter: Oh bravo, Monsieur! I see that sir has an excellent knowledge of Français. It's like being back home.

Man: Are you taking the mick?

Waiter: Oh no! You keep it up, Monsieur. Please make yourselves comfortable. (They sit.)

Waiter: Let me give you our menu. I think you will find it has everything that your heart could possibly desire.

Woman: (Looking at menu.) Oh my God!

Waiter: You're too kind.

Man: It all looks very tempting.

Waiter: We aim to please. But perhaps you would like a small aperitif whilst you look through the menu?

Man: I haven't looked at the starters yet, but I'll have a drink.

Waiter: Un peu de vin?

Man: That's right – a pint of lager.

Waiter: And for Madame?

Woman: Oh, I don't know... what shall I have?

Man: Well, we are splashing out tonight.

Woman: In that case, I'll have a Taboo and black.

Man: Do you want a cherry?

Woman: Oh yeah, and have you got one of those umbrella things?

Waiter: I'll see what I can do. I shall just be un moment. (Goes to get drinks.)

(Couple study menus. Waiter returns.)

Woman: Have you got any specials?

Waiter: Ah – the specials! But of course! Perhaps, Madame, as a starter, I could recommend the 'Poids de Luste'. I think you will find that it will really... how do you say... get you going.

(Man and woman become increasingly lustful.)

Man: Doesn't take much to get her going...

Woman: (Gazing at waiter.) You look extremely tasty... I mean, that sounds very tasty!

Man: Is it me or has it suddenly got very hot in here?

Woman: We'll both have it.

Waiter: Excellent choice. I'm sure you will be most satisfied.

(Couple flirt embarrassingly.)

Waiter: Ahem! (Couple return to normal.) If you are ready to move on, I would suggest our 'Acces d'angere'. (Couple become increasingly angry and argumentative.) They are absolutely...

Man: Look, if you know what's good for you, you'll stop flirting with my girlfriend!

Waiter: Oh, pardon, Monsieur, I was just...

Woman: Don't 'pardon' us, you arrogant pig! Come on, we're leaving.

Man: Where are our coats?

Waiter: Shall I take that as a 'yes', then?

(Couple return to normal.)

Man: Oh yeah, we'll have two. I'm a bit stuck what to have for main course, though.

Waiter: Well, have you seen what they're eating over on the next table? (Couple become envious of next table.)

Woman: Oh, that looks loads better than what we're having.

Man: Yeah! That looks fantastic. I wish we were having their dinner.

Woman: Go and grab the plate off them.

Waiter: No need, Monsieur. I will bring both of you some 'Les yeux d'envie' of your very own.

(Couple return to normal.)

Woman: Thanks very much. What shall we have next?

Waiter: Everything we offer is equally enticing.

(Couple become increasingly arrogant.)

Man: I'm not being funny, mate, but if you're talking about cooking, mine is the business. I mean, all this stuff on the menu is a pile of dog food in comparison, isn't it?

Woman: Yeah. Apart from me, you're the best cook I know. I'm not being big-headed, but my 'Téte plein d'arrogance' is unbeatable.
(She mispronounces it.)

Waiter: 'Téte plein d'arrogance'.
(Waiter corrects pronunciation.)
I am quite sure Madame and Monsieur are both excellent chefs,
(Couple return to normal.)
and I only hope that what we present to you is at least sufficient for your needs.

(Pause, then couple become covetous)

Man: Oi! waiter! I want that! I don't care what it is – I want it! As long as it isn't too expensive.

Waiter: Ah, that would be the 'Désire de gain'. I would love to have that myself.

Woman: Well, you can't, because I'm going to have it.

Man: I noticed it first, so it's mine!

Waiter: This is not a problem. I will get it for both of you.
(Couple return to normal.)
Can I tempt you to anything else?

Man: I'm not bothered.
(Couple become apathetic.)
Whatever.

Waiter: But I need to know so that I can order it for you.

Woman: What's the rush? Just chill out, will you...

Man: Yeah. Come and grab a seat or something.

Waiter: I'll put both of you down for the 'Puissant Bothere', yes?

(Pause.)

Man: Do what you want. I'm not interested.

Waiter: Madame? (Pause.) Madame?
Two 'Puissant Bothere'
(Couple return to normal.)
Anything else?

Man: I'll tell you what
(Couple become greedy.),
we'll have everything.

Waiter: Everything?

Woman: Yeah, everything. And hurry up,
because I'm starving. Do us
a favour, will you? Pass us the
leftovers from that table.

Waiter: That would be the
'Greede Totallement'.
Are you sure you can eat all that?

Both: Yes!

Waiter: Excellent. (Couple return
to normal.) So if I can read
back your order...

Man: And speak in English, I can't
understand a word of what
you're saying, Pierre, or
whatever your name is.

Waiter: Pas de probleme...
Excusez-moi – Excuse me.
(During this speech, the
couple respond to each 'dish'
by acting out the sin.)
You will start with the
'Loads of lust', then the
'Fits of anger', the 'Envious eyes',
moving on to the 'Headful of
arrogance', the 'Desire to have',
the 'Can't be bothered',
and finishing with the
'Totally greedy'.
May I congratulate you on
your choices?

BIBLE

JAMES 1:14,15 (WE ARE TEMPTED TO SIN BY OUR EVIL DESIRES)

....

QUESTIONS

IN THE SKETCH WHAT DOES EACH DISH REPRESENT?

ACCORDING TO THE MESSAGE IN THE SKETCH, IF WE GIVE IN TO TEMPTATION WHAT IS THE RESULT?

WHAT PRACTICAL STEPS CAN WE TAKE TO AVOID GIVING IN TO TEMPTATION FOR EACH OF THE EVILS DEPICTED IN THE SKETCH?

Woman: Just bring us what we want.

Waiter: Certainly. Bon appetit. (Off stage, waiter calls.)
Oi Satan, you're gonna love this, they've only
gone and ordered the whole lot.

THE PARABLE OF THE UNFORGIVING SERVANT

CHARACTERS

1 – the unforgiving servant
2 – the master, forgiving
3 – in debt to character 1

PROPS

None

ADDITIONAL INFORMATION

Contemporary setting; location can be anywhere appropriate.

1: Hi – sorry I'm late.

2: That's all right.

1: Er, look... about the money. Basically I got up this morning, got my cheque book –

2: Don't tell me – just as you were writing the cheque, your dog walked across your cheque book, did a poo, then skidded across the room on it. That was the last cheque book you had, and you can't get a new book till next week.

1: Oh no, I just went to the bank and –

2: And just before you got there, a big gang of Mexican bandits attacked you, saying (Adopts a Mexican accent.), 'We don't need no stinkin' badges,' stole all your money, and swapped it all into potatoes.

1: No! Look, I know I promised I'd have it for you today, but this time next week, I won't let you down. I promise.

2: Come on – how long has this been going on?

1: I don't know... a month or two?

2: Nearly a year.

1: All right, a year, then. What if I pay you back so much a month – what d'you think?

2: We've already tried that. You said you'd pay me £20 a month, then £10 a month, then £5, then a pound, then 50p – I'll be dead before I get my money back!

1: Look, I don't have the money, okay? Here, take this ring – it was my Gran's, so it's worth quite a bit.

2: I don't want your ring.

1: All right, what about this coat? It's very warm.

2: I don't want your coat, either. Anyway, it's mine.

1: Oh. What about my boots then?

2: Definitely not.

1: Why?

2: They stink!

1: Well, what do you want?

2: Look, just forget it, will you.

1: What? Our friendship?

2: No, not the friendship – the money!

1: Eh?

2: Just forget it. Our friendship's far more valuable than some stupid money.

1: What?

2: I'm wiping the slate clean.

1: You're what?

2: From now on, you don't owe me a penny.

1: Oh, I can't just... you mean... I can't believe it! All of it? Hey, I owe you one!

2: Yeah – a big one. (2 exits as 3 enters.)

1: Oh, hello.

3: All right?

1: No, I'm not all right. What happened to that fiver you owe me?

3: Well, I –

1: Don't come up with some stupid excuse, I want it back, and I want it now!

BIBLE

MATTHEW 18:21-35

QUESTIONS

WHAT IS WRONG WITH CHARACTER 1'S ATTITUDE?

IN THE PARABLE, WHAT DOES JESUS SAY WILL HAPPEN TO THOSE WHO DON'T FORGIVE OTHERS?

WHAT DOES FORGIVING SOMEONE 'FROM YOUR HEART' MEAN (VERSE 35)?

CHARACTERS

Character 1 – a bit of a lad and an old mate of Character 2
Character 2 – one of the lads. He's recently become a Christian and is hesitant to speak up about his new faith.
Holy Spirit

PROPS

Four pint pots

ADDITIONAL INFORMATION

This sketch is set in a pub. The Holy Spirit can be played on stage but only seen by Character 2, or can be a voice off stage. It is important that Character 1 does not interact with the Holy Spirit.

Two's

Character 1:	Fancy another pint?
Holy Spirit:	Don't you think you've had enough?
Character 2:	Get lost, will you!
Character 1:	You what?
Character 2:	Er, I said 'Get lots' – I'm dead thirsty.
Character 1:	Yeah, well you can 'get lots' when it's your round not mine, all right? (Goes to get drinks.)
Character 2:	Look, stop embarrassing me in public!
Holy Spirit:	What's the problem? Can't face the truth?
Character 2:	Don't start preaching now, okay?

Holy Spirit: Oh, I'm sorry, I didn't know I had to follow a timetable.

Character 1: (Returning with drinks.) There you go.

Character 2: Oh, stop being so high and mighty!

Character 1: Well, excuse me! I didn't realise buying you a pint was such a crime!

Character 2: What? Oh, I didn't mean you.

Character 1: Well, who did you mean, then?

Character 2: Er, me – I should've got the drinks in.

Character 1: Yeah, you should have. Hey, have you seen that new girl behind the bar?

Character 2: Yeah, you can't help seeing her in that excuse for a skirt!

Holy Spirit: You shouldn't have been looking.

Character 2: I wasn't looking, actually.

Character 1: Not much! I saw you order that diet Coke just so she had to bend down!

Holy Spirit: Don't remind me.

Character 2: Stop hassling me, will you?

Character 1: All right, all right, I'm only having a laugh. It's just you and me, remember?

Character 2: That's what you think...

Character 1: What d'you mean?

Character 2: Nothing.

Character 1: You know, you're acting really weird tonight. In fact, you've been acting really weird ever since you started going to that 'God squad' thing.

Holy Spirit: Now's your chance to tell him.

Character 2: No way!

Character 1: Yeah, you have. I mean, you don't hang out with the lads anymore, you don't get hammered, you don't even swear, for God's sake!

COMPANY

Holy Spirit: Say something.

Character 2: I don't know what to say.

Character 1: What d'you mean?

Holy Spirit: Tell him.

Character 2: I just can't.

Character 1: Why not?

Holy Spirit: Do it!

Character 2: Give us a chance, will you.

Character 1: Look, what is up with you?

Holy Spirit: Come on!

Character 2:	Just leave it, will you!
Character 1:	Oh, be like that then.
Holy Spirit:	Let me say it for you.
Character 2:	Okay, I will.
Character 1:	Fine.
Character 2:	Right...
Character 2 & Holy Spirit:	(Together.) I've become a Christian.

Character 1:	You what?
Character 2 & Holy Spirit:	(Together.) I've become a Christian. Is that a problem?
Character 1:	What? You? You've been suckered into that load of rubbish?!
Character 2 & Holy Spirit:	(Together.) It's the best thing that's ever happened to me, actually.
Character 1:	Yeah? Well, I need a drink. Same again?
Character 2 & Holy Spirit:	(Together.) No thanks. I'm not thirsty anymore.
Character 1:	Fair enough. (Goes to get drink.)

BIBLE

GALATIANS 5:25 (Keeping in step with the Spirit)
ZECHARIAH 4:6 (God's work flows from his Spirit not our effort)

....

QUESTIONS

How would you describe the relationship between Character 2 and the Holy Spirit?

When is Character 2 in and out of step with the Holy Spirit?

Can you think of examples in your life when you've been in and out of step with the Holy Spirit?

CHARACTERS

Woman – young, pleading her innocence to her partner
Man – suspects his partner is cheating on him
Jesus – understanding, strong

PROPS

None

ADDITIONAL INFORMATION

Young couple experiencing problems in their relationship. They ignore Jesus' offer of perfect love.

UNFORGIVEN

Woman: Forgive me.

Man: I can't.

Jesus: I can.

Woman: Why not?

Man: That's a stupid question, even by your standards.

Woman: I said I was sorry, didn't I?

Man: Yeah? Well, saying sorry's easy.

Woman: What do I have to do, then?

Jesus: Nothing. Just believe in me.

Woman: Excuse me, this is a private conversation. Look, I know you're annoyed with me, but I didn't even do anything.

Man: You didn't do anything? You must think I'm a total idiot. I heard what happened.

Woman: Oh yeah? And who told you?

Man: What –

Woman: Come on, who told you?

Man: What difference does that make?

Woman: No, don't tell me. Your mate 'Mr. Reliable'.

Man: Hey, don't make matters worse by blaming him.

Jesus: I've already taken the blame.

Man: Do you know that bloke or something?

Woman: Look, it's all just a misunderstanding, believe me.

Man: Why should I?

Woman: Because you said you loved me.

Man: Yeah? Well, we all make mistakes, don't we?

Woman: Oh, so one minute you'll do anything for me, and the next you don't even want to know me?

Jesus: I know how that feels.

Man: Have you ever even bothered to think how this makes me feel?

Woman: Well, I –

Man: No, of course you haven't.
Do you ever think about
anyone but yourself?

Jesus: I do.

Woman: If selfishness was a qualification,
you'd have a degree by now!

Man: That's right. Turn this round
so it all seems like my fault.
That is so typical of you!
I may not be perfect, but at
least I'll admit it.

Woman: Oh well done! So what do
you want? A prize or something?

Man: Stop being such a drama queen!

Woman: I'm not, but you're not taking
the slightest bit of notice of
what I'm saying!

Jesus: I'll listen.

Man: You could punch that bloke in the face, then I'd take notice of you!

Woman: So now you want blood, do you?

Jesus: Sometimes it's the only way.

Man: Just butt out, will you?

Woman: Look, I'm being honest. That's the only way we can sort this out.

Jesus: I'm the way.

Man: You wouldn't know the truth if it smacked you in the face!

Jesus: I'm the truth.

Woman: Get a life, will you.

Jesus: I'm the life.

Man: Who are you?

Jesus: Who do you say I am?
(Pause, Jesus moves into the background.)

Man: Jesus.

Woman: I'm glad he's gone. (Pause.) **Look, I am sorry.**

Man: I know.

Woman: So will you forgive me?

Man: No.

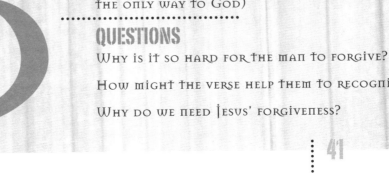

BIBLE

JOHN **14:6** (JESUS IS THE WAY, THE TRUTH AND THE LIFE –
THE ONLY WAY TO GOD)

QUESTIONS

WHY IS IT SO HARD FOR THE MAN TO FORGIVE?

HOW MIGHT THE VERSE HELP THEM TO RECOGNISE JESUS?

WHY DO WE NEED JESUS' FORGIVENESS?

CHARACTERS

God – friendly, accommodating but always firm and sure. Never arrogant
Presenter – arrogant, self absorbed, insincere
Stage Manager – efficient, professional

PROPS

2 chairs, clipboards for presenter and stage manager

ADDITIONAL INFORMATION

Takes place in a TV studio. God is best played as a voice off stage, but can be on stage if preferred.

Stage Manager:	And in 5... 4... (Mouthed.) 3... 2... 1... (Points to camera.)
Presenter:	Good evening, and tonight on The Word I'll be continuing my series on freak phenomena by having a chat with 'The Big Cheese' – the Almighty himself! So put your hands together for the man at the end of the prayer line, please welcome... God! (Applause.) Thanks very much for granting us an audience with yourself.
Voice of God:	No problem – it's a pleasure to be here.
Presenter:	So 'Almighty'... if I can call you 'Almighty' – or maybe you'd prefer something else?
Voice of God:	God's fine.
Presenter:	Right then. God. Father. Son. Holy Spirit. Sounds like you're a pretty busy guy.
Voice of God:	You could say that.
Presenter:	Although I think it's fair to say you don't seem to have done very much for quite a while...
Voice of God:	What do you mean?
Presenter:	Well, you claim to have made us, right?
Voice of God:	Right.

Presenter: But then it seems you pretty much left us to it. I mean, I know you rested on the seventh day, but just how long a break do you need?

Voice of God: Actually, I couldn't be busier.

Presenter: Well what I mean is, there's not much evidence of you being around.

Voice of God: But I'm here, aren't I?

Presenter: So?

Voice of God: So I've always been here.

Presenter: In fact, come to think of it there's not much evidence of you at all!

Voice of God: Really?

Presenter: Yeah… I mean, as far as I know, you might not even be here – you could be wishful thinking. I could be hallucinating. I could be talking to an empty chair.

Voice of God: Or maybe I'm really here.

Presenter: Are you sure? 'Cause I'm certainly beginning to wonder. Anyway, we'll come back to that. Now answer me this: where do you actually live?

Voice of God: Everywhere.

Presenter: But you seem to concentrate your living in nice suburban areas – I mean we don't see much of you in Africa, for example. Or maybe you just don't care about starving children.

Voice of God: A father gives his children a table full of food, and then leaves them to share it out.

Presenter: Not quite with you on that one, God, but I'm sure there's logic in there… somewhere. So tell me – why do you think people find it so difficult to believe you're there?

Voice of God: Because they refuse to listen when I speak.

Presenter: (Pretends not to hear God.) Pardon?

Voice of God: Because…

Presenter: Only joking, 'Your Mightiness', go on.

Voice of God: People can see me if they want to, they just don't want to.

Presenter: Who said that? (Laughing.) Only joking – just having a bit of fun.

Voice of God: That's the problem.

Presenter: Eh? Ah, now that IS the problem. What is your problem with people having fun?

Voice of God: Nothing – I invented it.

Presenter: Then for your sake, let us have some! I mean all these rules – no sex, no drugs, no rock and roll. Surely it's up to us what we do?

Voice of God: Of course, it's your choice.

Presenter: Exactly. It's our life, so let us live it.

Voice of God: Or not.

Presenter: Eh? Look, if we can just finish off where we started. If you really are there, how am I supposed to know? You could be a figment of my imagination, a product of my sad and demented mind, or... in fact, what am I talking about? You don't exist!

Voice of God: Prove it!

Presenter: No, you've lost me again there, 'Your Wiseness'. Anyway, thanks for turning up – if you did – I mean, who can tell? And at the end of the day, who cares? Well, good luck proving yourself God, and maybe next time we'll get chance to find out what you're really like. Well that's all from me tonight. Thanks again to God, if he's not already left, or maybe he was never here? Like I said, who can tell? Good night, and may the chair be with you.

Stage Manager: And in 3... 2... 1... and clear. Go to break. (Presenter exits.) Sorry about that, God.

Voice of God: Don't worry, I'm used to it.

BIBLE

JOB 38:2.3 (Who are we to question God?)

QUESTIONS

What is the interviewer's attitude towards God?

According to the passage, what would God's attitude be towards the interviewer?

If you had the opportunity to ask God one question what would it be?

ED WOOD

CHARACTERS

Tony – old school, club circuit ventriloquist.
Ed – the ventriloquist's dummy. Mannerisms and voice of dummy at beginning which are lost when he becomes human.

PROPS

Chair for ventriloquist, big box for dummy, beer bottle, cigarette (real or imitation) and lighter

ADDITIONAL INFORMATION

The strength of the sketch rests on the actor's ability to clearly define Ed as the dummy and then Ed as human.

Tony: Good evening, ladies and gentlemen! My name is Tony Sparkles – ventriloquist to the stars, fresh from my world tour of the north-east coast of England. Thank you for inviting me back to this beautiful old auditorium, and have I got a show for you tonight!

(Muffled noise from box.)

Tony: Sorry about that. As I was saying, have I got a show for you tonight!

(Muffled noise again.)

Tony: Excuse me a minute. What's the matter?
Ed: I want to come out and say hello.
Tony: Yes, but I remember what happened last time you came out to say hello, and so do all the ladies and gentlemen.
Ed: I know, but this time I'll be good, I promise.
Tony: Well, all right then, as long as you promise. (Opens box.)
Now then, let's get your leg out... (Lifts Ed Wood out.) **and sit you up.** (Sits him on his knee.) **Right. Say hello to all the ladies and gentlemen, Ed Wood.**

Ed: Hello, ladies and gentlemen.

Tony: And how are you today?

Ed: (Coughing.) Fine.

Tony: Are you all right?

Ed: Just got a bit of a splinter in my throat.

Tony: He-hey! You're funny! Now then, what have you been up to today?

Ed: Visiting my folks.

Tony: Don't think I know them.

Ed: No, but you must've heard of them.

Tony: Why's that?

Ed: They're very poplar.

Tony: He-hey! You're funny! Anyway, I've got something special for you. What's this?

(Tony pulls out a bottle of beer.)

Ed: A gottle of geer.

Tony: Come on, Ed Wood, you'll have to do better than that, they can't hear you at the back! What's this?

(Silence.)

Tony: Talk, then.

Ed: I don't want to. I'm bored.

Tony: Oh dear, I think someone's in a bit of a bad mood today. What's the matter?

Ed: This.

Tony: What about it?

Ed: Everything.

Tony: But Ed Wood –

Ed: And that's another thing – it's a stupid name. I mean, I don't call you Gepetto, do I? I want to be called something cool like Steve or Romano.

Tony: All right, then, Romano, what d'you want to do now?

Ed: I want to walk.

Tony: Walk?

Ed: Yes. You made me, so you could teach me.

Tony: Well, all right, but it's going to be tough.

Ed: I know, but I can do it with your help.

Tony: Okay. Let's start by standing you up. (Ed falls over.) Are you all right?

Ed: Nothing a hacksaw and some sandpaper can't sort out.

Tony: He-hey! You're funny. (Tony helps Ed Wood up, trying to steady him.) **Now, you need to put your weight on your legs.** (Ed starts to fall again.) Oh, it's not going to work.

Ed: No, let me have another go. (Ed Wood finds his feet and stands unaided.) **Look! I'm standing!**

Tony: He's standing ladies and gentlemen! (Claps and encourages audience to give Ed Wood a round of applause.) **Very good. Now you need to move your left leg forward.** (Moves left leg forward.) **Concentrate – keep looking at me. Now your right leg.** (Moves right leg.) **Keep looking at me.**

Ed: It hurts.

Tony: I know, but you can do it. Just keep looking at me.

Ed: Look! I'm walking!

Tony: He's walking ladies and gentlemen! (Claps and encourages audience to give Ed Wood a round of applause) **Keep looking at me.**

Ed: I don't need to anymore – I can do turns! (Ed turns in circles. As he turns the third time he loses all his mannerisms and his voice becomes human and sarcastic.) **Well, that was easy enough. Thanks very much.** (Ed lights a cigarette that he gets from his pocket.)

Tony: What're you doing?

Ed: What does it look like, genius? I'm smoking a cigarette.

Tony: Don't! Please, it's dangerous!

Ed: Yeah, yeah. Blah, blah, blah. Look, Grandad – sorry, Tony. I'll do what I want, okay? (Drinks from the beer bottle.)

Tony: Now what are you doing?

Ed: Are you thick or something? I'm drinking a gottle of geer (He says it mockingly.) **Anyway, see you.**

Tony: Where are you going?

Ed: Away from you.

Tony: But Ed Wood – I mean, Romano. Don't play with fire.

Ed: Look, I'm not stupid, you know.

Tony: So what about me?

Ed: What about you? Sad loser!

(Ed leaves – sound of flames and screaming.)

Ed: (Off stage.) **I'm burning. Help me Tony. I'm burning!**

BIBLE

GENESIS 2:7 (GOD MADE THE MAN FROM DUST AND BREATHED LIFE INTO HIM)
ECCLESIASTES 11:9 (GOD WILL JUDGE US FOR THE WAY WE LIVE)

QUESTIONS

AT WHICH POINT IN THE SKETCH DO ED WOOD'S PROBLEMS START?

HOW ARE THESE BIBLE VERSES ILLUSTRATED IN THE SKETCH?

WHAT CAN WE LEARN FROM ED WOOD'S EXPERIENCE?

CHARACTERS

Angel 1 – professional, efficient hit man
Angel 2 – unprofessional, inefficient hit man
Human – terrified, not a Christian

PROPS

Angel 1: black sunglasses, radio ear piece and mouth piece, gun
Angel 2: black sunglasses, radio ear piece and mouth piece, megaphone, gun, bag containing photos and information disk
Human: dressing gown
Chair and television

ADDITIONAL INFORMATION

The sketch is set in the human's home.
This sketch should be played fast and pacy.

JUDGEMENT

(Human enters, switches on TV, sits down and nods off. Angels enter.)

Angel 1: Freeze!
Angel 2: (Through megaphone.) **Move away from the chair!**
Human: But he just said 'freeze'!
Angel 2: (Through megaphone.) **Freeze... and move away from the chair!**
Human: How am I supposed to do that?
Angel 2: (Through megaphone.) **Right, forget it. On the floor... on your knees... do a press up... lift your leg in the air... sing the national anthem... louder... louder...**
Angel 1: Stop making him do that.
Angel 2: (Through megaphone.) **What?**
Angel 1: (Grabbing megaphone.) I can hear you!
Angel 2: What? Oh – sorry.
Angel 1: (Into mouthpiece.) Target secured.
Human: What about my rights?
Angel 1: You haven't got any!

Human: What?

Angel 1: You have no right to remain silent and no right to speak. Everything you have said, done and thought has been used in evidence against you.

Human: What?

Angel 1: You have no right to remain silent and no right to speak –

Human: You what?

Angel 2: He said don't speak.

Human: But I haven't –

Angel 2: Don't speak.

Human: But I only –

Angel 2: Don't speak.

Human: I –

Angel 2: Don't speak.

Angel 1: Do you mind?

Angel 2: Sorry.

Human: Sorry... Wait a minute, no I'm not! This isn't fair – I haven't done anything!

Angel 1: Really?

Human: Yeah! I was just watching Friends, fell asleep for five minutes, and then you two burst in.

Angel 2: Oh great, Friends. I love this one.
(Sits down engrossed in TV.)

Angel 1: Do you mind? We've been sent to do a job.

Angel 2: Wilco! (Goes back to TV.) Oh, this is the one where Joey gets married to Phoebe...

Angel 1: (Snatches megaphone and shouts down it.) Oh really!

Human: How do you know that? This is a new series!

Angel 1: We know everything.

Human: Really? Hey, do Ross and Rachel end up together?

Angel 2: Well, what happens is...

Angel 1: PLEASE can we get on!

Angel 2: Freeze!

Angel 1: We know everything because we have the information.

Human: What information?

Angel 2: All of it.

Human: All of what?

Angel 2: The information.

Human: What information?

Angel 2: All of it.

Human: All of what?

Angel 2: The information.

Human: What information?

Angel 2: All of it!

Human: All of what?

Angel 2: The information!

Human: What information?!

Angel 1: Look, this is taking far too long. Stop playing dumb.

Angel 2: Sorry.

Angel 1: Not you – her! We know everything because we have the information.

Human: What information?

(Angel 2 pulls disk out of bag.)

Human: What's that?

Angel 1: The informa.. Oh, forget it! It's everything we need to know, OK?

Human: Like what?

Angel 1: Like everything you've ever said, everything you've ever done, everything you've ever thought.

Human: That's impossible!

Angel 2: Believe me, we know everything.

Human: What 'everything'?

Angel 2: Everything! Smart, eh?

Human: Well, I don't believe you.

Angel 1: You don't have to, your beliefs aren't important anymore.

Human: You're lying.

Angel 1: Really?

Human: No one's got that kind of technology.

Angel 1: (Receives message in ear piece.) **OK... yeah.** (Opens bag and throws photos on floor. Human moves forward to look.) **Back up!** (Points gun.)

Human: Hang on a minute, these are all pictures of my life.

Angel 1: We know.

Angel 2: (Points to a photo.) **That's when you got hammered on the stag night, snogged the waitress and got thrown out for doing the salsa on the salad bar!**

Angel 1: Thank you!

Angel 2: Sorry.

Human: I want to see some ID.

Angel 1: Tough.

Human: I want to make a 'phone call.

Angel 2: Too late.

Human: I want to see my solicitor.

Angel 1: You haven't got one.

Human: I've got a really bad itch!

Angel 2: Scratch it!

Human: I want...

Angel 1: What you want is no longer important. You made your choice – time's up.

Human: So what now?

(Both angels receive a message in their ear pieces – they nod to each other and aim at the back of the human's head. Blackout. Gunshots.)

BIBLE

MATTHEW 24:42-44 (No one knows the day the Lord will come)

••••••••••••••••••••••••••••••••

QUESTIONS

What is the purpose of the angels' visit?

How might the Bible verse have been of help to the human in the sketch?

How might the sketch differ if the angels came to visit you?

CHARACTERS

Man – Jack the Lad, weakens under the increasing weight of sin
Sin – everyone's best mate, becomes increasingly pushy, controlling and dangerous

PROPS

Beer bottle, pills, condoms, knife

ADDITIONAL INFORMATION

Initially everything seems fun for both the man and the audience, then sin takes control changing everything.

DEVIL ON YOUR BACK

(Man enters through the audience with Sin on his back – sin remains there throughout the sketch – both are laughing.)

Man: I never!
Sin: Yeah you did – I was there, remember?
Man: All right, I admit it, but it was your fault!
Sin: Couldn't have done it without you. Hey, look at that geek over there...
Man: Where?
Sin: (Pointing.) There, with that sad haircut.
Man: Oh yeah, what a loser!
Sin: Hey, what about his friend, though...
Man: Cor! All right, darlin'? What're you doing with him?
Sin: Maybe she needs glasses, eh?
Man: Or maybe she's never met a real man!

(They laugh.)

Sin: Make a good team, don't we?

Man: The best!

(Man squirms a little.)

Sin: What's up with you?

Man: Nothing, I'm fine.

Sin: Can't take the pace?

Man: Course I can! What's next?

Sin: Whatever you want. Here – have a little pick-me-up. (Puts a pill in his mouth.)

Man: Thanks.

Sin: Hey, how about another session with the lads – always a laugh, innit?

Man: (Squirming more.) Er, yeah... I guess.

Sin: We could play 'Pint or puke' again, eh?

Man: Well, I –

Sin: Or how's about blowing some more cash down the bookies – bound to get lucky this time.

Man: (Stumbling.) Ow! Get off a minute, will you?

Sin: No, I'm comfy here. Besides, what would you do without me, eh?

Man: I know we have a laugh and stuff, but –

Sin: But what?

Man: I dunno. Maybe I could –

Sin: Take up knitting? Join the Scouts? Wear tank tops? Help old ladies? Have a –

Man: (Getting up.) Okay, okay, just don't push it, all right?

Sin: As if I would... Hey!

Man: What?

Sin: Let's have some serious fun.

Man: What d'you mean?

Sin: (Moving arm around his neck and opening a lager in his face.) **Drink this.**

Man: (Spluttering.) **I don't want –**

Sin: (Throwing tablets in his mouth.) **Take these.**

Man: (Choking.) **Wait a minute –**

Sin: (Stuffing condoms in his pocket.) **Use these.**

Man: (Falling.) **But I –**

Sin: (Punching him on the right.) **Take this!**

Man: (Falling further.) **Aagh!**

Sin: (Punching him on the left.) **And this!**

Man: (Falling further.) **Aagh!**

Sin: (Stabbing him in the heart.) **And not forgetting this!**

Man: (Collapsing.) **Aagh!**

Sin: I don't know what you're complaining for.

Man: (On his knees.) **Get off me!**

Sin: I mean, you chose me.

Man: Let me go!

Sin: And I've given you everything you wanted.

Man: No!

Sin: So it's only fair that I get paid for a job well done, isn't it?

(Man dies screaming as Sin laughs.)

BIBLE

ROMANS 6:23 (THE WAGES OF SIN IS DEATH, BUT GOD'S GIFT IS ETERNAL LIFE IN JESUS)

QUESTIONS

HOW DOES THE RELATIONSHIP CHANGE BETWEEN THE MAN AND SIN THROUGHOUT THE SKETCH?

LOOKING AT THE VERSE, HOW DOES THE INTRODUCTION OF JESUS AFFECT THE CONSEQUENCE OF SIN?

HOW WOULD YOU REWORK THE SKETCH IF YOU REPLACED THE SIN CHARACTER WITH JESUS?

CHARACTERS

Prisoner – is becoming aware they are about to die. Experiences all the relevant emotions
Jesus – compassionate, strong, very real
Guard – professional, efficient and unemotional

PROPS

Coat for the prisoner, electric chair, two chairs

ADDITIONAL INFORMATION

The prisoner is awaiting execution. Jesus appears in contemporary clothing (he's not actually a cleaner). The execution is most effective when strobe lighting effects and sound effects are used.

(Jesus is sitting on a chair.)

Prisoner: (To the audience.) **Hey! Gimme a smoke! I said gimme a smoke! You pigs!** (Kicks the chair towards Jesus.)

Jesus: Don't.

Prisoner: Who the hell are you?

Jesus: A friend, I'm a friend.

Prisoner: Well have you got a smoke, 'friend'?

Jesus: Sorry, I don't smoke.

Prisoner: So what do you do?

Jesus: Clean. I'm the cleaner.

Prisoner: Yeah? (Spits at him.) **Well, you missed a bit.**

Jesus: No, not that sort. I get rid of people's mistakes.

Prisoner: Oh right, like Harvey Keitel?

Jesus: Sort of. People screw up, if they ask me, I'll sort it out.

Prisoner: So are you offering your services?

Jesus: It depends.

Prisoner: Yeah? On what?

Jesus: Have you screwed up?

Prisoner: Well, I'm in here aren't I?

Jesus: What did you do?

Prisoner: (Draws chair close to Jesus.) I crossed the road, when the sign said 'Don't walk'. (The girl laughs.)

Jesus: I'm being serious.

Prisoner: What's it to you?

Jesus: I can't help you unless you talk to me.

Prisoner: I need a smoke.

Jesus: Those things will kill you.

Prisoner: So what? I'm dead anyway!

Jesus: No. There's still time.

Prisoner: For what? For my dreams to come true?

Jesus: Possibly.

Prisoner: Don't mess with me.

Jesus: I'm not.

Prisoner: They'll be here for me soon.

Jesus: I know, but there's still time. What did you do?

CLEANER

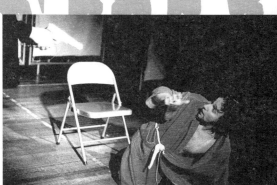

Prisoner: I got caught.

Jesus: So why should I help you?

Prisoner: What do you mean?

Jesus: You broke the law.

Prisoner: Yeah, and who hasn't? They just didn't get caught.

Jesus: They will. Do you want me to help you, or not?

Prisoner: How can you? It's too late.

Jesus: There's still time.

Prisoner: I'm scared.

Jesus: I know.

Prisoner: I don't know what happened really...

Jesus: Go on.

Prisoner: I just lost control. I didn't mean to do it... any of it.

Jesus: (Quietly.) **Yes you did... all of it. Didn't you? Didn't you? Didn't you?**

Prisoner: OK. So I did. But now I'm sorry. (Falls on knees and cries.) **Oh God, I'm so sorry.**

Jesus: Give me your coat.

Prisoner: What for?

Jesus: It's time. (He takes the coat.) **Now go... go.** (The prisoner runs off)

(Jesus puts on the coat. Guard enters and straps Jesus in the electric chair.
Jesus is electrocuted and cries out in agony.)

BIBLE

JOHN 5:24 (YOU HAVE CROSSED FROM DEATH TO LIFE IF YOU HEAR AND BELIEVE IN JESUS)

QUESTIONS

WHY DOES THE CLEANER TAKE THE PRISONER'S PLACE?
AT WHAT POINT IN THE SKETCH DOES THE 'CROSSING OVER', REFERRED TO IN THE VERSE, BEGIN?

THE ELECTRIC CHAIR REPRESENTS THE CROSS. TAKE A FEW MOMENTS TO IMAGINE WHAT IT MUST
HAVE BEEN LIKE FOR JESUS AS HE HUNG ON THE CROSS.
THEN THANK AND PRAISE HIM.

Woman: Now, in order to expand this area,
we need to break through here,
thus leaving ample space for your
mobile toys...

Man: What?

Woman: Just a little joke – I was in fact referring
to your vintage cars, all ten of them!

Man: Thirteen.

Woman: I beg your pardon?

Man: I've got thirteen.

Woman: Ah, that's unlucky – I thought you had ten.

Man: Well, business is booming...

THE
OF THE

Woman: Ah well, not to worry.
We'll delay construction and
alter the dimensions slightly.
Unless, of course, you'd consider
displaying three of them on
your drive? (Man begins to
shake his head.) **No, quite.**
I just thought that since it's
three miles long... Er, I'll talk
to the builders this afternoon.
Shall we move on?

Man: What's this?

Woman: Oh, they're the sculptural columns for the leisure area.
With such extensive alterations, we felt it was appropriate to go the
whole hog and give it a completely new look. What do you think?
They'd look great by the poolside, really compliment the tiles.
I thought quite Gaudi.

Man: Gaudy, very gaudy.

Woman: Er, no. Gaudi, Mr. Jones.

Man: Eh?

Woman: Gaudi – one of the most celebrated architects of all time.
Surely you're familiar with his work?

Man:	No.
Woman:	The Great Cathedral in Barcelona, perhaps?
Man:	No.
Woman:	A wonderful structure, set against the backdrop of...
Man:	Belch!
Woman:	There is one concern, though. The width and height of the columns could present illumination difficulties.
Man:	What?
Woman:	Light.
Man:	Yes please.
Woman:	What? Oh, right. (Lights his cigar and coughs.) Now, where were we?
Man:	Light.

PARABLE
RICH FOOL

Woman:	No thank you, I don't smoke... Oh – light! Well, for a marginal cost, we could solve this problem with several skylights.
Man:	Tobago nut?
Woman:	Er, no thank you.

(Man starts coughing, which increases.)

Woman:	They're very popular with the stars, you know... (She laughs.) **Very popular with the stars? Skylight – stars? Oh, didn't you see the connection, Sir? Sir? Would you like to see the extensions for the rest room?**

(Man dies coughing.)

BIBLE

LUKE 12:16-21

QUESTIONS

WHAT WAS THE PROBLEM WITH THE MAN'S ATTITUDE IN THE SKETCH AND IN THE BIBLE PASSAGE?

WHY IS MATERIALISM AND HAVING EVERYTHING NOW SO TEMPTING?

HOW CAN WE GUARD AGAINST THIS TEMPTATION AND BE 'RICH TOWARDS GOD'?

A Winters Tale

CHARACTERS

Jeremiah – outdated geek, desperately trying to be cool, short-tempered, talks with a lisp
Boy – cheeky, troublesome, school-age
Girl – a bit dizzy, outspoken, school-age

PROPS

Bike, jar of coffee wrapped as frankincense, plastic gold, something wrapped as myrrh

ADDITIONAL INFORMATION

The sketch is set in a youth club. Both the girl and boy should be buzzing with energy.

Announcer: Ladies and gentlemen, please put your hands together and welcome Jeremiah Killjoy!

Jeremiah: Woof! Woof! Woof! Hey there kids, how's it hanging out? Safe and sorted!
Yes, I'm Jeremiah Killjoy or JK as my posse like to call me. Thanks for inviting me along to your youth club today. Anyway, I've been asked to tell the story of the first Christmas. Now many people ask, 'But what was the first Christmas really like?' Well, it all began with...

(Enter boy on BMX)

Jeremiah: ... an idiot riding his bike over the cables. Oi!!

Boy: What?

Jeremiah: (Aside.) Don't worry - I've got a way with 'yoof'. Get off that bike, sit over there, shut up and listen!

Boy: Tuh!

Jeremiah: Now, where was I? Ah, the first Christmas. Now, it all began with a voice from heaven saying...

(Enter girl.)

Girl: Hey, give us me fags back, you!!

Jeremiah: Shut up! (Composing himself.)
If you're staying, stay. If you're going, go quickly!

(Girl sits next to boy.)

Jeremiah: Now, where was I?

Boy: The first Christmas.

Jeremiah: Thank you. Yes, the first Christmas. Now, the voice from heaven said, 'Mary, thou shalt be laden with child, and –'

Boy: So she was up the duff then?

Jeremiah: Yes, with the Lord's child.

Boy: Oh aye!

Jeremiah: What do you mean, 'Oh aye'?

Girl: Well, it's a bit weird, innit? This 'voice' turns up out of nowhere and tells some girl she's pregnant with a lord's baby. As if!!

Jeremiah: I know, I know, it's an amazing story, isn't it?

Boy: Oh, so it's not real then?

Jeremiah: Yes, of course it's real.

Girl: But you just said it was a story.

Jeremiah: So? I could tell you a story of when I was a student, and I took part in this crazy sponsored twenty-four hour three-legged fancy dress litter pick in Milton Keynes, and that would be real!

Boy: No, that would be boring.

Jeremiah: Anyway, Mary and her 'partner' Joseph chose to spend Christmas in Bethlehem that year.

Boy: (Interrupting.) Ibiza shut then, was it?

Jeremiah: But when they got to the inn, they couldn't get in.

Girl: So why was it called an 'in' then?

Jeremiah: Look, it could have been called The Wagon and Horses for all I care, but the point is that it was full, so they had to go to a stable.

Boy: Where they kept the horses.

Jeremiah: What?

Girl: For the wagons.

Jeremiah: Yes... anyway, in the meantime, three wise men arrived after looking at the stars.

Girl: I'm a Capricorn.

Boy: Why didn't they just look at the road signs if they were so wise?

Jeremiah: And lo! They entered the stable bearing gifts.

Girl: What gifts?

Jeremiah: Well, what would you like for your birthday?

Boy: Thought you said it was Christmas?

Jeremiah: Yes, the child was born at Christmas.

Boy: That's unlucky, cos I bet he only got one lot of presents.

Jeremiah: (Sighing.) So, what would you want?

Boy: Pringles, a four-pack and 20 B&H.

Girl: Yeah, you owe me some fags.

Jeremiah: Or how about gold, frankincense and myrrh.

Girl: Oh, very handy!

(Boy grabs the gold.)

Jeremiah:	Oi! What are you doing with that?
Boy:	(To girl.) Look, it's gold.
	(The gold snaps in half.)
Girl:	You've broken the gold – you're gonna get done!
Boy:	It's not real, it's plastic.
Jeremiah:	(Snatching back the gold.) Thank you! Now, moving on swiftly, the frankincense was actually –
Girl:	(Unwrapping it.) A jar of coffee.
Jeremiah:	The frankincense was actually to represent the ointment used to anoint kings and the myrrh was a scent used to disguise the smell of dead bodies.
Boy:	I'd have stuck with the Pringles.
Jeremiah:	Later, the shepherds arrived –
Girl:	With their dogs.

Jeremiah:	What?
Girl:	Well, shepherds always have dogs, don't they?
Boy:	And Land Rovers.
Jeremiah:	Look the point is that they arrived after hearing about the new birth.
Girl:	Who told them?
Jeremiah:	The voice.
Boy:	That voice gets around, dunnit?
Jeremiah:	And so they celebrated the birth of the baby Jesus.
Girl:	So, what happened to him then?
Boy:	Well, he's dead now, isn't he.
Jeremiah:	No, no, he's alive!!
Girl:	Oh right, so he's about 2,000 years old, is he?
Jeremiah:	Yes, because this little baby was a special little baby – he was the Son of God
Boy:	(To girl.) Did he just say, 'thumb of God'?
Jeremiah:	Son, Son, the little boy!! He was the Son of God who came to earth to die and then rise again so our sins can be forgiven, just like it says in the Gospels.
Boy:	What's a 'Gospel'?
Jeremiah:	Anyway, it only leaves one question to ask and leave you with: Who's going to be your 'Christmas Number 1'?

(Boy and girl name pop singers vying for the Christmas number 1 slot.)

Jeremiah:	Thank you and goodbye!

BIBLE

MATTHEW 1:18 – 2:12 (The birth of Jesus)

....

QUESTIONS

What is wrong with Jeremiah Killjoy's approach?

According to the passage, what are the amazing events surrounding the birth of Jesus?

Take time to reflect on who is Number 1 in your life.

60

UNUSUAL SUSPECTS

CHARACTERS

Robert – repeat offender, arrogant
Johnson – detective inspector, determined, tough
Lever – detective constable, silent but strong presence

PROPS

Table, two chairs, jug of water, two cups,
pair of handcuffs with key

ADDITIONAL INFORMATION

This sketch takes place in a police interview room.
Robert is determined not to give anything away.
Johnson adopts a range of strategies, from aggressive
to passive, to get a confession from Robert.

(Robert and DC Lever on stage. DI Johnson enters.)

Johnson: Interview time: 9.37am. Present: DI Johnson, DC Lever, and the accused, Robert Jones. Okay, let's get the formalities over with, shall we? Right, Mr. Jones, you have the right to remain silent, but anything you say may be used as evidence against you. Well, Robert, we're going to have to stop meeting like this – people are starting to talk. (Looking through notes.) It's not a bed of roses, is it? Nice, you've really excelled yourself this time. Your mum must be so proud.

Robert: She's dead, actually.

Johnson: And probably spinning in her grave as we speak. Anyway, enough pleasantries, let's get down to business. So, if you could tell us in your own words, what happened? (Silence.) Look, Robert, telepathic conviction has never been my forte. Let's have it in simple English, shall we?

Robert: Can I have a glass of water?

Johnson: Certainly, Robert. Anything to loosen those vocal chords. (Lever pours a glass of water, spits in it and hands it to Robert.) **Better?** (Robert pushes it away.) **Oh, I'm sorry, did you want ice and lemon? Look, we can do this the easy way or the hard way. You know, someone once told me that all things come to those who wait, but I've never been known for my patience. In your case, though, I'll make an exception. You see, I'm happy to wait... and wait... I'll sit here for as long as it takes, and when it's all over, you're going down.** (Silence.) **Look, Robert, the evidence is black and white – we all know you're guilty. It's very simple: you confess and we can all go our separate ways.** (Silence.) **Three words, Robert, the first word sounds like...**

Robert: Oh look! I did it, all right?

Johnson: For the record, Mr. Lee, you admit to being guilty as charged?

Robert: It was never in dispute, was it?

Johnson: No, not in your case.

Lever: (Pager beeps.) Er... can I have a word, Ma'am?

Johnson: Yes?

Lever: In private.

Johnson: (To Robert.) **Don't go away.**

Robert: (Hold up cuffed hands.) Well, I'll try not to.

(Johnson and Lever step aside.)

Johnson: What is it?

Lever: You're not going to believe this. I've just got a message through. He's only gone and dropped all the charges. We can't hold him on anything now.

Johnson: (Johnson and Lever both move back.) **Well, Robert, looks like it's your lucky day, it seems like he's dropped all the charges.**

Robert: (Getting up.) Well that's me, then.

Johnson: Sit down! I haven't finished with you yet. (Pours some water.) In fact, let's have a toast to your freedom – guilty as sin one minute, and walking free the next. So, what did you do, then? **I SAID WHAT DID YOU DO?** Did you threaten him, Robert? No one just drops all the charges! After all you did to him, you're telling me he's prepared to forget the lot? Come on Robert, you and me are old friends. You can tell me. What did you do?

Robert: Simple.

Johnson: Really?

Robert: Yeah. I just apologised to him. (Robert holding up hands, Lever undoes cuffs.)

BIBLE

ACTS 2:38 (REPENT AND BE BAPTISED IN THE NAME OF JESUS FOR FORGIVENESS)

QUESTIONS

WHAT IS THE MOST SIGNIFICANT LINE IN THE SKETCH, AND WHY?

THE VERSE CALLS FOR REPENTANCE (TURNING AWAY FROM SIN), WHY IS THIS IMPORTANT?

IN THE BIBLE, REPENTANCE MEANS MORE THAN JUST SAYING SORRY.

IN YER FACE ARE EVANGELISTS WHO
DELIVER A SWIFT KICK TO THE HEARTS
OF OUR AUDIENCE THROUGH THE MEDIUM
OF THEATRE. WE ARE ARMED WITH A
MESSAGE THAT IS AS BEAUTIFUL AS LOVE
AND AS HARD AS THE CROSS. WE ARE ALL
PROFESSIONAL ACTORS WHO USE OUR
SKILLS TO PROCLAIM THE LIFE CHANGING
NEWS OF JESUS CHRIST. WE DIG DEEP,
ALWAYS LEAVING GOD'S FOOTPRINTS IN THE
RICH SOIL OF THE MIND.

WHO WE ARE

WE PRODUCE THEATRE TO GLUE YOUR
SOUL TOGETHER – ALWAYS PROCLAIMING
THE TRUTH OF JESUS CHRIST CRUCIFIED
AND RISEN. OUR SHOT-TO-THE-HEART
STYLE OF DRAMA ENCOURAGES YOUNG
PEOPLE TO THRUST THEIR HANDS INTO THE
WOUNDS OF CHRIST FOR THEMSELVES.

WE OFFER EVANGELISTIC SHOWS, WORKSHOPS
AND SEMINARS FOR YOUTH GROUPS,
CHURCHES, PRISONS, NIGHT CLUBS AND
ANY OTHER SUITABLE VENUES. WE ALSO
LEAD WEEK-LONG RESIDENCIES IN
SCHOOLS WHERE WE TAKE ASSEMBLIES,
DRAMA AND RE LESSONS. GIVE US A
PLATFORM AND WE'LL TREAD IT, BUT HOLD ON
TIGHT THE ONLY HANDRAIL TO GRASP WILL
BE THE GOSPEL!

WE WORK WITH YOUNG PEOPLE OF 11 YEARS
AND OLDER. WHILST WE ARE BASED IN
CHEADLE, NEAR MANCHESTER AND HAVE A
HEART FOR THE NORTH-WEST, WE ALSO WORK
ALL OVER THE COUNTRY AND HAVE BEEN TO
PLACES AS WIDESPREAD AS HIGH WYCOMBE,
OXFORD, CUMBRIA, REDCAR, SUFFOLK,
LINCOLN AND KENT.

FOR MORE INFORMATION PLEASE CONTACT:

Karen Arnold (Administrative Director)
In Yer Face • Mill House • Mill Lane • Cheadle • Cheshire • SK8 2NT
TELEPHONE: 0161 491 3090 E-MAIL: inyerface@domini.org
WEB: www.inyerface.org.uk

WE LOOK FORWARD TO HEARING FROM YOU SOON.